ZHANGJIAJIE

Majestic Mountains of Hunan, China

ZHANGJIAJIE
Majestic Mountains of Hunan, China

Photographs by Sun Jianhua

Times Editions
Marshall Cavendish

CONTENTS

INTRODUCTION

MIRACULOUS ZHANGJIAJIE

While China has many other mountains and valleys that are more significant in terms of magnitude or established fame, Zhangjiajie nonetheless remains a remarkable landmark in its own right. Its development as a tourist resort began only as recently as 1980, but even then early attempts to showcase its natural attractions met with quick success. As a visitor was famously inspired to proclaim, "This is a precious pearl lost in the deep mountains!"

Today, Zhangjiajie has truly captured the hearts and imagination of millions of visitors who travel far and wide to bask in its rocky charm. Its many accolades include a litany of grand and poetic titles, which translate from Chinese as Natural Museum, Monument to the Nature, Strangest Mountain under the Heaven, Devil Expeller of Mountains, Miniature Fairland and Enlarged Potted Landscape, amongst other inspired monikers.

Zhangjiajie's reputation rests largely on the Wuling Forest of Mountains, made up of landforms that are truly unique in this world. Scattered over the 264 sq. km of the central region, known as Wulingyuan, are 3,103 natural stone erections that each stand over 100 metres tall. These stone formations are laid out in evocative patterns, and contrast against the traditional mountain ranges and their uniform walls and peaks. It is indeed incredible that rock formations take such humanoid shapes, inspiring writers to liken them to an army of stone soldiers standing shoulder to shoulder, or a procession of monks on their way to prayer.

These elements have made Zhangjiajie a haven for nature lovers, who make pilgrimages here from distant lands. A Japanese painter who visited Zhangjiajie for inspiration once commented with deep emotion: "I previously thought that scenes in Chinese paintings all existed only in the imagination. It is only now that I realise China does indeed have such spectacular scenes that are part of the natural landscape. Zhangjiajie is an enormous Chinese painting in itself!" Professor Wu Zheng-yi, the famous Chinese geologist, goes further to claim: "Zhangjiajie must truly be the sole original inspiration for all Chinese landscape paintings."

In 1979, Wu Guan-zhong, a contemporary painter was persuaded to visit Zhangjiajie Tree Farm, now Zhangjiajie State Forest Park, to capture its beauty. He was initially unwilling to make the journey, but his attitude changed and his mood lifted once he entered Zhangjiajie. As he faced the peculiar stone mountains, he recalled thinking: "Zhangjiajie Tree Farm excited me beyond expectation. It is like a precious pearl lost in the mountains, until it came to be finally recovered by me."

Thus moved, in January 1980 he published his article, *Zhangjiajie: A Lost Pearl of Scenery*, to share his newfound love for Zhangjiajie with the world. In this piece, recognised as the first work to formally introduce Zhangjiajie to the outside world, Mr. Wu was so moved by his subject matter that he could not help waxing lyrical in his descriptions. He wrote:

"I do not understand the geological value of the continuous and condensed stone mountains. The cliffs poke into sky. The stone mountains are erect like vertical lines. The horizontal lines with all their twists and turns are also very intriguing. The interlocking lines are like an exquisite piece of art. More accurately, they manifest a sense of deep structural beauty. They can even be called a masterpiece of painting, in themselves. To seek natural beauty for my paintings, I have laboriously covered many famous mountains. My observation is that none of Yandang, Wudang and Qingcheng can ever match the beauty of this unknown Zhangjiajie."

Even foreigners could not help expressing their awe. In September 1989, the then-Assistant Governor of Colorado State in the USA, Nancy Dick, visited Zhangjiajie after hearing how it had often been compared to the Grand Canyon. Ms Dick spent two days in Zhangjiajie. When it was time for her to leave, she graciously noted in a farewell entry: "Zhangjiajie is fabulous. It is very peculiar. People say that the Grand Canyon is miraculous. In my opinion, Zhangjiajie is even more beautiful. This is the most beautiful place in the world."

Those who ponder the magnificent ridges and peaks might wonder how they came about. Professor Chen Guo-da, an internationally renowned scholar in geology, has published a thesis wherein he indicated four stages for the geological evolution in the area of Zhangjiajie, namely, "quartz" (the preliminary stage for material accumulation); "quartzite" (the formative stage); "surfacing the horizon", and "the carving of ridges and peaks". In his view, the entire process of formation would have lasted a staggering 1.5 billion years. According to his theory, severe crust movements in northwest Hunan about 1.5 billion years ago, caused large amounts of granite magma to gush out to the surface along with the quartz. The accumulation of quartz led to the formation of quartzite, until around 380 million years ago when the area started to subside.

Severe crust movements circa 200 million years ago caused weathering (i.e., rocks cracking as a result of chemical, physical and biological battering and decay), erosion (i.e., the mixture of water and sand chiseling the rocks to carve out gullies and ravines), and gravitation (i.e., rocks with an unstable center of gravity). These processes slowly sculptured the landscape into the magnificent line of ridges and peaks we observe today.

These mountains have been given names and even inspired numerous legends and mysteries. The Couple's Rock is one example. At first glance, they appear to be two ordinary-looking peaks. On further scrutiny, the peaks resemble the heads of a man and woman: one bigger than the other; one ruggedly outlined while the other is smoothly delineated; one laughing wildly while the other timidly bows her head. Amazingly, one can make out what appears to be a row of teeth set into the husband-rock's face.

Just as the Couple's Rock makes for a memorable sight, the Peak of the Anticipating Bride has its fair share of fans. From afar, the peak resembles the silhouette of a bride with long hair cascading down over her shoulders. However, if you continue to walk and observe it from different angles, you will successively identify the physical resemblance of a young lady, a middle-aged woman, and finally an old lady. This feature is made even more intriguing due to the stonewall opposite it, which sports a tiny but visible hole. Imaginative speculators have thus extrapolated that the young bride must be in a constant state of eagerness and craving, in wanting to look through the stonewall for a peek at her imaginary other.

Below its glorious skyline, the territory has many scenic spots that are favoured by different visitors for the views they command and the adventures they offer. In fact, it is a miracle that such an astounding number of natural beauties are contained in such a relatively small area of 9,516 sq. metres. To name but a few: the Yellow Dragon Cave remains one of the most beautiful caves in the entire country; Mount "Gate to Heaven" has been likened to the Soul of the Entire Area; River Mao Yan is dubbed the "Gallery of Hundreds of Miles;" the Cave of "Nine Heavens" is a contender for the Greatest Cave in Asia; and Lake Jiang Ya has earned itself the nickname "Water World". The potential for tourism is so great that the rock known as "Magic Needle", within the Yellow Dragon Cave, has even been insured for over 100 million yuan, the first instance of its kind in the Chinese tourism industry. Mount "Gate to the Universe" has hosted an international stunt-flying competition, wherein a man made a successful flight through the cave. This historic event has been acknowledged by the Guinness World Records.

Though there is little agricultural activity , the gorgeous streams that run through the area feed a rich and diverse ecology of plant and animal life. Even as early as the 1980s, naturalists sighted such first-tier "protected animals" as the South China tiger, leopard and red-bellied pheasant; as well as second-tier species such as macaque, pangolin, black bear, otter and salamander. The red-bellied pheasant is perhaps the most frequently encountered inhabitant of this area. The small bladder hanging down its neck has caused this little creature to be nicknamed the "carrying-water chick" by locals, because it visits the creeks every four or five days to store around 200 grams of water in its bladder.

The botany of Zhangjiajie is just as renowned, with over 870 varieties making up 107 families of plant life; a significant number as it is almost four times that in Europe. Among the 19 rare plants, the dove tree is perhaps the most famous as an example of a "living fossil". Though this piece of natural heritage survived the Glacier of the Fourth Period circa 2.5 million years ago, botanists were unable to locate it until the mid-nineteenth century. In the National Preserve of Mount Ba Da Gong, a river bend has been renamed "Dove Tree Bend" after the 10,000 odd dove trees that grow along its banks. It is here that the world's biggest surviving specimen, the "King of Dove Trees", continues to grow. It rises 30 metres, has a diametre of 1.5 metres, and its canopy covers 600 sq. metres.

As if these marvels are not enough, Zhangjiajie is also a significant heritage site. The earliest human activities here can be traced back 100,000 years to the Paleolithic Age. Even in the earliest written records of Chinese civilisation, Zhangjiajie was already featured as a favoured place to visit. Folktales include how the mythical God of Agriculture lived a reclusive life here long ago, and how 3,000 years ago the Emperor of Shun exiled a rebel warrior and confined his movements to this area.

Perhaps the most romantic of tales involve how the place earned its name. Zhang Liang, the first Prime Minister of the Western Han Dynasty (206 B.C–25 A.D.) died while visiting the area and was buried here. The place was henceforth named Zhangjiajie, meaning the "boundary of Zhang family," after the Prime Minister. Another significant scenic spot, the "Yellow Stone Village", takes its name after his mentor, Father Huang Shi, whose name translates as "yellow stone."

For a long time, these stories were dismissed as little more than folklore. In recent years though, Chinese historians and archaeologists have been able to trace many of the aforementioned personalities, and corroborated much credible evidence of the area's historical heritage. In a declaration signed by 28 scholars and specialists during a symposium held in December 2002, Zhangjiajie was officially recognised as "a region abundant with historical legacies and cultural tradition". This has inspired tourists to visit the territory's many sanctuaries such as the Pu Guang Buddhist Temple, the Mount Wu Lei Taoist shrine, as well as the Palace of Plum Blossoms.

Like other remote regions, Zhangjiajie is also home to various ethnic minorities. Among the 1.57 million native population in Zhangjiajie City, about 1.1 million people are from the Tujia ethnic group. Their history can be considered both old and young, depending how one views it: "old" in the sense that its recorded history goes back over 3,000 years, but "young" as their ethnic group was only recognised in 1956.

As a minority group, the Tujia suffered severe oppression at the hands of their rulers, and were caught up in many rebellions. In 47 A.D., Emperor Liu Xiu of the Eastern Han Dynasty sent Marshall Ma Yuan to deal with the Tujia rebels, but he was unable to tame the passionate Tujia forces. In 1370, Emperor Hong Wu of the Ming Dynasty allocated 200,000 troops to suppress a rebellion led by Qin Hou, a Tujia native in Yong Ding County, Hunan Province. Indeed, governors and administrators of various dynasties failed in their efforts to tame the region. Stability was only achieved when they wisely left the respective chieftains to manage their people.

For all their ferocity, though, it would be unfair to stereotype Tujia natives as unruly rebels. The Yujia have also defended the land when it was under the threat of foreign invasion. During the reign of Emperor Jia Jing in the Ming Dynasty (1368-1644), China was threatened by Japanese warriors in the southeastern coastal areas. Tens of thousands of Tujia soldiers were conscripted to fight the Japanese invaders, and they achieved two major victories within two months. Tujia soldiers also participated in the Opium War (1840-1842) against Western invaders. General Sun Kai-hua, himself a native of Tujia, led troops to fight the French navy in Taiwan and managed to significantly stall the invasion attempt. As a result, Emperor Guang Xu wrote a lengthy eulogy praising his courage, and extolled his loyalty to the imperial court of the Qing Dynasty (1616-1911).

Zhangjiajie became historically prominent again during the Communist Revolution in the early years of the twentieth century. On 2 April 1928, General He Long returned to his base in Sang Zhi County, Hunan Povince, and inspired an uprising, which served as the groundwork for the Hunan-Hubei-Sichuan-Guizhou Revolutionary

Base and the renowned "Second Regiment" of the Red Army. Peasants in the area who joined the Red Army included illustrious veteran generals like Ren Bi-shi, Guan Xiang-ying, Wang Zhen, as well as the 100,000 martyrs who sacrificed their lives in battle. In November 1935, the Second and Sixth Regiment of the Red Army held a swearing-in ceremony before setting off for the Long March to northwestern Shaanxi Province. Chairman Mao Ze-dong was duly appreciative, and praised their patriotism.

Given the Tujia's energetic lifestyle and culture, it is not surprising their customs and arts are so colourful and captivating. From food to architecture, music and choreography to social custom, these remain utterly unique and impressive. Their cuisine is characteristically sour and spicy, to aid digestion. The music and choreography comprise lively mountain songs and hand-waving dances, of primitive simplicity yet displaying a high degree of symbolic sophistication. Foreigners are typically intrigued by their ethnic customs, especially what they call the "crying marriage." During the wedding ceremony, a singer performs sad songs which inspire merry-makers to share the bride's melancholy over having to leave her household. Performed long enough, tears will start to roll all around.

Zhangjiajie has also been proclaimed the "Home of Wushu and Qigong" (i.e., Martial Arts and Breathing Exercises). Du Xin-wu, a native of the area, was known as the "Master of the South" during the Republican Era (1911-1949), after he defeated numerous Japanese bushido champions. He also served as the personal bodyguard for Dr. Sun Yat-sen, the founding father of Republican China. In the 1980s, internationally renowned qigong master named Zhao Ji-shu joined many state missions abroad, and even returned with an award from the King of Belgium.

Since the implementation of economic reforms and growth of tourism in the 1980s, Zhangjiajie has experienced a brisk pace of modernisation. In 1982, the State Council declared the inauguration of Zhangjiajie National Park, the first national park in China. In 1988, the City of Zhangjiajie was established to further develop local tourism. The central government also invested over 10 billion yuan to improve local infrastructure, especially transportation and telecommunication. Today, a network of air, rail and road links has taken shape steadily and connects the area to over 30 domestic cities by air and 20 by express buses. The telecommunication system links the territory with the world via broadband Internet. Within this space, there are about 400-odd hotels, capable of accommodating nearly 40,000 tourists, and over 30 travel routes that add up to 400 km in total. The annual number of visitors increased from 500,000 in 1982 to 7.8 million in 2002, and has since gone on to exceed 10 million. Accordingly, the city has been awarded such honorary titles as "the 40 Best Tourist Resorts in China", "the Nationwide Renowned Tourist Area", "China's Excellent Tourist Cities", "the National 4A-Class Tourist Region" and "National Geological Park" among others. In 1992, Wulingyuan was recognised as a World Heritage Site by UNESCO, and thus, Zhangjiajie officially became a world-class tourist attraction.

Such is Zhangjiajie, a land that never ceases to amaze.

GETTING THERE

Zhangjiajie lies in the northwest region of Hunan Province, and has been increasingly visitor friendly since it was added to UNESCO's World Natural Heritage list. Tourists can catch a two-hour flight to Zhangjiajie from any of China's larger airports. There are several daily departures from international gateways such as Shanghai, Beijing and Hong Kong. Though the train route takes a much longer time, it is an interesting alternative for the colourful sights that one can view along the way. One can also catch a bus from the province capital Changsha; this 400 km journey takes a day.

Map of Hunan Province

GEOLOGY AND LANDFORMS

A clump of loose sand can be transformed into a hard rock. A hard rock can be carved into an exquisite piece of art. Both these processes are dependent on the passing of time. Over time, the ancient geology in this region has slowly but surely grown to manifest its own sophisticated beauty.

(opposite) Many of the mountains and geographical features have been given names. This rock face is known as "Painting of the Old Geology".

(above) Breaking the water surface, the rocks sitting in this riverbed appear to be solidified crystals floating on the water.

(opposite) This beautiful natural stone arch is known as "A Historical Step Over 380 Million Years".

(above) The effects of weathering have created cracks and crevices in the rock face, giving these mountains an air of mystery.

(opposite) The mountains of Zhangjiajie make for striking pictures. Accordingly, viewing platforms have been contsructed at key scenic areas.
(above) The sheer variety of flora and fauna that grow in the area means that each season brings forth new views and landscapes.

(above) The golden rays of the sun give these mountains the semblence of copper.
(opposite) This feature named "Splendid Memory" rises from the ground like a pair of fingers.

(opposite) Although there are many peaks among the mountains, some are particularly outstanding because of their height.
(above) The slopes and valleys in the area are covered by an abundance of lush natural vegetation.

NATURAL SCENERY

Someone once likened the sight of Zhangjiajie to a surreal dream. Another person called it an illusion of Heaven. Indeed, the breathtaking sight of quartz sand mountains is doubtlessly something to remember for a long time to come. Its precise impression, though, is something mere words can never do justice to. Instead, one needs to view this in person to appreciate the strength of its profound beauty.

Zhangjiajie State Forest Park

Zhangjiajie's application to be recognised as the first National Forest Park in China was approved by the State Counsel in 1982. Prior to this, the park was known as the Zhangjiajie State Tree Farm. The park is made up of various quartzite mountain landforms, and is famous for its breathtaking mountain ranges, tranquil valleys, curious rock shapes and beautiful waters. Forests cover 97% of the area, and are rich in vegetation, exotic flowers and herbs, and unusual trees. Rare birds and animals also make their home here. The main scenic spots are: Huangshi Village, Golden Whip Brook, Sand Knife Valley, Yuan's Land and Sparrow Hawk Village. Huangshi Village and Golden Whip Brook are the more popular tourist stops.

(above) The Pigeon plant has pretty white flowers.
(opposite) The park is located northwest of Wulingyuan.

Huangshi Village

Located in the western part of Zhangjiajie Forest Park, Huangshi Village lies 1,200 metres above sea level. According to legend, this was where Father Huangshi, teacher of the famous marquis Zhang Liang of the Han Dynasty, spent many years in secluded meditation. The place was named after him, although Huang also means "yellow" and Shi also translates as "stone" in the Chinese language. Huangshi Village is the largest single scenic destination in Zhangjiajie, and has inspired the saying: "Without visiting Huangshi Village, one has not visited Zhangjiajie". The main attractions in the vicinity are: Six Wonder Pavilion, Pick Star Platform, Five Finger Peaks, Front Garden, Left Towers to the Sky Bridge, Monkey Marshall Commands His Soldiers and Golden Turtle Searching the Sea. There are also many scenic spots within Huangshi Village itself.

(opposite) Sunrise at Huangshi Village

(above) The rocky outcrops rising from the ground have been likened to giant bamboo shoots pointing skywards.

(opposite) Huangshi Village takes on an ethereal feel due to its high elevation in the mountains.

(opposite) The locals have named this feature "Three Friends in Winter".

(above) The area has a long winter season with average temperatures hovering around 3 to 4 ° Celsius.

(opposite) "Jade Vase Mountain" is the name given to this solitary pinnacle.

(above) Translated from the Chinese, this area is known as "Monkey Marshall Commands His Soldiers".

(opposite) Low cloud cover in the high altitudes means that the higher peaks are shrouded in a sea of mist.
(above) In autumn, lush green plants take on a different look as they shed their leaves.

(above) Snow falls in the area from late January to early February.
(right) Travelling by cable car gives visitors an overview of the area.
(opposite) Autumn is the best season to visit Huangshi Village as the weather is the most pleasant at this time.

Golden Whip Brook

Golden Whip Brook takes its name from the famous Golden Whip Rock located further upstream. The brook itself is 6 km long, and meanders from west to east along the peculiar mountains and deep valleys. The area's scenic beauty has inspired poetry and paintings alike, with numerous notable locations that include: Golden Whip Brook, Flower and Fruit Mountain, Cut Mountain to Save Mother, Scholar Star Rock, Purple Grass Pool, Meeting from Thousand Miles Away and Fish Jumping Pond.

(above) Golden Whip Rock rises 380 metres high and is a prominent landmark in the area.
(opposite) This view from the riverbank is called "Welcome Guests at the Boudoir Gate".

(above) Wild Lotus Flower **(opposite left)** Lobster Flower **(opposite right)** Monkeys are attracted to the fragrance of the flowers.

(opposite) Golden Whip Brook meanders for a distance of 7.5 km

(above) Changes in the ground level have created mini "Water Mushrooms" along the brook.

(above) Pebbles along the river bed cause the stream to form unique water ripples.
(opposite) As the leaves change colour in Autumn, the land takes on a different look.

(above) The entire region is visitor friendly and rest areas such as these have been constructed to cater to tourists.
(opposite) The sun's rays filtering through the mountains throws the spotlight on simple rocks.

Yuanjiajie

Yuanjiajie is located in the northern sector of Zhangjiajie State Forest Park. It forms a platform above the Sand Knife Valley and main scenic spots include: No. 1 Bridge under Heaven, Enchanting Platform and Back Garden.

(above) This splendid view is just one of the 110 scenic spots that can be sighted in Yuanjiajie.

Sparrow Hawk Village

Sparrow Hawk Village is located in the southeastern sector of Zhangjiajie State Forest Park, and lies 5 km from Lao Mo Wan. Above the village is a long and narrow ridge that offers high ground from which to examine the surrounding lands. The area is famous for its majestic and perilous cliffs. Other scenic spots nearby include Sky Bridge and Imposing Tower with Layers of Rocks.

(opposite) This feature is called "Cut with an Axe".

(above) An unusual perspective of the cliffs as seen through the canopy of the trees.

Yangjiazhai Scenery

Yangjiazhai is located in the northwestern part of the Wulingyuan region. Quartzite landforms cover 3,400 hectares. The scenery is grand and tranquil, with scenic spots that include: Fragrant Stream, Tianbofu, Black Dragon Village, Sky within One Step, Sky Corridor and Ape Dread Rock.

Tianzishan Nature Conservatory

Tianzishan is one of the three central scenic regions in the Wulingyuan area. It lies in the northwest, stretching from Zhangjiajie in the south to Suoxiyu along its eastern fringe. The area is named for Xiangwang Tianzi, the tribal chief who once led his Tujia people in a revolt against their overlords. Tianzishan is a land of high plateaus, from which one can gaze out for many kilometres into the distance. The total area covers 67 sq. km, and includes both a commanding sight of the mountain ranges, as well as encounters with the four wonders of Tianzishan: misty clouds, moony nights, beaming rays and shiny snow. The main scenic spots include: Imperial Pen Mountain, Fairies Present Flowers, He Long Park, Knight Trains the Horses, Thousand Layers of Rocks, Commanding Platform, Bay at God's Hall, Huge View Platform, Farm in the Sky and Gathering of Divine Soldiers.

(opposite) In winter, the trees turn white and make for a most beautiful picture.
(above) Frost and ice on the leaves creates the illusion of jade trees with crystal branches.

(above) In autumn, the mountains take on a warm, rusty glow.
(opposite) The area takes on a frosty feel when it is winter.

(opposite) This solitary peak is known as "Hermit".

(above) The magnificent view gives the impression that you are looking at a Chinese painting.

(above) Red Azaleas in bloom add colour to an otherwise green landscape.

(opposite) Locals believe that this view is a scene from heaven.

(top) Cable cars link the peaks at Tianzi Mountain.

(above) Kiwi fruit are just one of the many species of plants growing in the area.

(right) Frozen branches and stems give the appearance of a crystal world.

(above) The name given to this structure is "South Sky Pillar".
(opposite) This view gives the impression that the mountains are floating in a sea of clouds.

(above) The frozen branches give visitors to the area a nice fresh feeling.

(opposite) The red berries manage to grow despite the cold and create a colour contrast against the white.

(above) The locals have given names to many of the scenic views and this one is called "Fairies Come into the World".

(opposite) If you look closely, you may be able to see why this feature is known as "Fairies Present Flowers".

(above) A close-up of the frozen vegetation which gives a feeling of purity.

(above) The gold of autumn leaves looks beautiful set against the clear blue sky.

(above) As the sun sets, the mountains take on a mix of light and shadow.

(opposite) When it snows, this feature known as "Knight Trains the Horses" is especially prominent.

(above) Seen in black and white, the view of Tianzi Mountain appears to be a waterfall of clouds.
(opposite) Depending on the weather and season, the mountain peaks may sport dense cloud cover.

(above) This collection of mountains has been named the "Gathering of Gods" by locals.

(opposite) At dawn, the skies take on vibrant shades of reds and oranges that are simply beautiful.

(above) As the weather moves from winter to spring, hints of green peak out from the drab landscape.
(opposite) This view has been called "Sail" as it gives the impression of a boat on water.

(opposite) This rock is called "Million Years Date".

(above) From the viewing platform, visitors can enjoy magnificent views such as this.

(above) The locals call this feature "Going to the Fairyland".
(opposite) Coniferous trees stand tall along the mountain slopes.

(above) The name of this waterfall translated from Chinese into English is "Wash Silk Threads in the Jade Pool".

(opposite) Interesting shadows are cast as the sun's rays filter through gaps in-between the mountains.

Suoxiyu Nature Conservancy

Suoxiyu is located in the eastern sector of Wulingyuan. Zhangjiajie lies to the west and Tianzishan is in the north. It has a total area of 147 sq. km, and is the largest among the three central scenic regions. According to the County Records of Cili dating back to the Ming and Qing Dynasties, the name "Suoxiyu" was inspired by the many rope-like streams in the area ("suo" means rope). The region's landforms only took shape during the relatively later stages of geological development, and this has resulted in a scenery that appears drastically different from that seen elsewhere in Zhangjiajie. Not only can one find peculiar clusters of stone mountains here, but there are also mysterious groups of limestone caves underground. Beautiful valleys and streams wind in various directions, while grotesque-looking rocks of different shapes and sizes jut out of the ground. The main scenic spots include: West Sea, Ten-miles Gallery, Water Surrounding Four Gates, Treasure Mountain Lake and Huanglong Cave.

(opposite) The mountains of Suoxiyu are seen in sihouette at dawn.

(above) Autumn casts a warm glow on this feature known as "Dragon Ridge".

(opposite) This mountain face is called "Song of Red Wall" after the natural colour of the stone.

(opposite) Due to its prominent location, this mountain is the first in the area to welcome each new morning.
(above) A wall of cliffs line-up in a row and appear to be in competition with each other.

Ten-Miles Gallery

Ten-Miles Gallery is a valley situated at the base of Tianzi Mountain. Walking in the valley gives one the impression of being in a gigantic art gallery filled with natural masterpieces.

(opposite) Seen against the sky, this rock resembles an "Old Man Gathering Medicinal Herbs".

(above) This traditional courtyard house has a tranquil setting with a lake in front and mountains surrounding it.

(above) This feature is called "Sky Steps with Hundred Dragons".
(right) These majestic mountains stand as silent monuments to the region's geological landscape.

(opposite) One of the landmarks in this area is this rock known as "Father and Son Protect the Treasures".
(above) "Asking the God" is another view that also features on visitors' must see lists.

Baofeng Lake

Baofeng Lake, located 1.5 km south of Wulingyuan City, is one of the better known scenic spots in the region. Its waters reflect the lush mountains surrounding it and the clouds to produce an enchanting effect. Visitors who go boating on the lake can glimpse landmarks such as Fair Lady Looking into the Mirror and Peacock Displaying its Fine Tail Feathers.

(opposite) Baofeng Lake is actually a man-made reservoir with multi-functions.
(above) A multi-tiered waterfall over Baofeng Lake is a striking feature.
(overleaf) The calm waters of the lake have a mirror effect and reflects the surrounding mountains.

(opposite) An ancient temple located deep in the mountains.
(above) The mountain and its reflection in the lake join seamlessly as one.

Zhangjiajie Rapids Drift

The Zhangjiajie Rapids has been designated by the General Administration of Sports in China as the official training base for rapids rafting. It is also the training site for foreign athletes competing in the 2008 Beijing Olympics. The rapids are indeed one of the most dramatic in the world, and are certainly matchless in Asia. In fact, rapids rafting at Zhangjiajie is such an exhilarating experience, many tourists brave the waters here just for a taste of the thrills. This area lies within the central Zhangjiajie and is one a favored destination with international tourists.

020
SHUN HANG
佛山市顺航安全装备厂
86—757—2813490

Drift in small three gorges, Loujiang River

These rapids lie in Cili County, 30 km east of Wulingyuan, and can be visited as part of a packaged tour of the eastern attractions. The river flows furiously in some parts but slows down to a tranquil crawl in others, as it travels through the lush valley. Visitors are seldom disappointed with the breathtaking views of the land around them, or with the sight of the sparkling water rushing by below.

Huanglong Cave

Huanglong Cave is located 10 km east of the Wulingyuan District government building, and is the most significant scenic spot in Wulingyuan. The interior covers more than 20 hectares and some sections are more than 160 meters wide, with the water going as deep as 15 km. The cave itself consists of four layers of rock. Two levels are underwater and two layers above the water level. The cave houses at least 13 spacious halls, 96 corridors, 3 waterfalls and an underground river. It is obvious, though, that there are clearly more wonders inside that have yet to be discovered. There are six particularly note-worthy spots, including Dragon Palace, Fairy Water and Sky Pillar Street. There are many rare stalactites, in various degrees of glitter and translucence, and which have taken the shapes of stone pillars, stone curtains, stone waterfalls, stone rivers, stone whips, stone flowers and other formations. Even the British Royal Geological Team that once explored this place proclaimed it to be one of the most dramatic limestone caves around the world, with every corner offering a feast for the eyes.

(above) This feature in the Huanglong Caves is called "Jade Bamboo Shoot in the Dragon Palace".

(right) With the aid of strategically place lights "The Golden Boy and the Jade Maiden" beckon all who enter the cave.

Jiutian Cave

Jiutian Cave (Nine Heavens Cave) is a most appropriate name for a natural cavern that has nine openings facing skywards. Situated at Futa Village, Sangzhi County, 70 km west of Zhangjiajie, the cave has a total floor area of 2.6 million square metres. Features within the cave include 40 large halls, 3 underwater rivers, 5 nature born bridges, 6 mountains, 7 small lakes, 8 "farmland', 10 waterfalls, numerous groups of stalactites and five spiral platforms of various heights. The enchanting wonders inside include Nine Star Mountain, Jade Palace, Crystal Palace, Palace of Mysterious Fairy from the Ninth Heaven and Palace of the God of Longevity.

(top) A panaromic view of Jiutian Cave.
(above) The cave floor resembles a typical field in a farm.
(opposite left) This feature is called "Give Tit for Tat".
(opposite right) With a shape resembling corn, this feature is known as "Stone Corn".

Loujiang River Scenic Region

Loujiang River Scenic Region is on the east line of the Zhangjiajie tour. It is next to the eastern part of the Wulingyuan core scenic zone. Within the region, people can view an enchanting scenery of lakes and mountains, visit beautiful gorges and cliffs, experience rapids and dangerous shoals while drifting on the river. The main scenic spots include Drift in Small Three Gorges, Loujiang River, the former residence of Du Xin Wu who held the title of the Chivalrous of South and North, warm springs and parachute jumping.

(opposite) A glimpse of the sky between two narrow valleys.

Tianmen Mountain State Forest Park

Tianmen Mountain (Mountain of Gate to Heaven) State Forest Park stands 10 km south of Zhangjiajie City. The ancient names for Tianmen Mountain are Cloudy Dream Mountain, Kettle Top Mountain, High Ridge Mountain and Jade Screen Mountain. In the sixth year of the Yong An period during the era of the Three Kingdoms, a big earthquake hit the mountain and created the Gate of Heaven. Thus the name of Tianmen Mountain came into being. Tianmen Mountain is 1,518 metres above sea level. Tianmen Mountain has unique natural views, including 16 mountains and 16 caves. The most famous of them, is Tianmen Hole. On 11 December 1999, a master pilot specialising in stunt flying flew through Tianmen Hole. He set a Guiness World Record when the plane flew through the natural mountain hole; the first time in history this had been achieved.

(above) Whether seen upclose or from afar, the mountains in the park are truly remarkable features that inspire awe from visitors.

Drift in Maoyan River

Drift in Maoyan River is on the west tour line of Zhangjiajie along the upper stream of the Lishui River, in Yongding District. The whole drift lasts for 50 km. With luxuriant trees, flying waterfalls and Tujia villages located along the riversides, the area forms a gallery of a hundred miles.

Eight Public Mountains State Natural Conservancy

Eight Public Mountains is located at the origin of the Lishui River, 89 km from Sangzhi County. Before the Qing Dynasty, the land and mountains in this area was divided among eight property owners. After these eight owners moved away, the area became public property. This was how the place got its name. It was declared a State Natural Conservancy in 1986. Within the 250 km region, the forest is so thick that sunlight can hardly penetrate. The streams are clear and water green and the air is very fresh. Many rare and endangered animals and plants are found here. This area is called the Gene Tank of Rare Species of the World, and is part of the Network of China Human and Organisms Conservancy.

HISTORY AND CULTURE

Zhangjiajie is home to over 20 different ethnic groups, each with its own history and unique cultural heritage. In addition to their colourful native costumes and unique architecture, the groups have unusual dances, special marriage customs and even traditional funeral rites.

PUGUANG BUDDHIST TEMPLE

Located at the city centre, the famous Pu Guang Buddhist Temple has a long history. It was constructed in the 11th year of the Yong Le Period of the Ming Dynasty. Since then, it has served as the Buddhist centre of the southern provinces and has hosted six conventions during which thousands of Buddhists were initiated into the religious order as monks or nuns. Pu Guang Temple is laid out in a very precise manner, and its structure reflects the traditional Chinese architectural styles of the Song, Yuan, Ming and Qing dynasties. The temple itself is made up of notable elements such ass the big gate, the second gate, Da Xiong Palace, Arhat Palace, Palace of Goddess of Mercy, Pavilion of the Jade Emperor, and so on. The temple has a very strong religious aura, and in 1959 was added to the list of Important Relics and Protected Spots within Hunan Province.

(opposite top) Daxiong Palace **(left)** Wenchang Temple **(right)** Wu Temple

大雄寶殿

履仁蹈義

Wulei Mountain

Wulei Mountain is located in the eastern part of Cili County. While the Taoists have long considered it to be a piece of sacred land, it is also rich in cultural and natural history. According to legend, it was here that Zhen Wu, the earliest practitioneer of Taoism, ordered the God of Five Thunders to despatch five thunderbolts, to help him battle a band of five evil dragons. It was thus that Wulei Mountain (or, Five Thunder Mountain) received its name. Over time, it earned a reputation as a Taoist stronghold, due to the many Taoist temples located here. Construction work on the local Taoist temples, houses and palaces started in the Yuan Dynasty, and were largely completed by the Ming era. Today, over 100 temples are still standing. These temples contain a total of 36 halls, 72 palaces and 48 villages. Wulei Mountain is next to Wudang Mountain of Hubei Province, which also boasts its own Taoist attractions. The most famous temple here is Golden Palace, where Zhen Wu the Great God is worshiped.

(opposite) A beautiful temple roof stands tall against the evening sun.

(above) Garden showcasing customs of the Tujia people.

(right) Dancers dressed in traditional costumes.

(opposite) The building known as the Fairy Pavilion of Nine Layers.

ANCIENT CITY OF JIUXIWEI

The ancient city of Jiuxiwei is located at Jiuxi Village, Jiangya Town in Cili County, east of Wulingyuan. The oldest buildings here date back to approximately 1390 A.D. According to historical records, "the City was constructed on the remains of Suokou Village of Song Dynasty. The city was 9 Li and 13 steps in circumference. It was 8 Zhang and 8 Chi tall with 4 gates, each with its own watchtower. Outside the north gate was a trench 480 Zhang wide. Outside the east, west and south gates was the Loujiang River, which also served as the city's moat." Today, all that remains are the south and north gates, some Ming Dynasty houses, and the stone-paved road in the city itself.

(top) Maidens dressed in traditional attire.
(above) The Plum Blossom Hall of Xingguo Temple.
(right) A typical street in Jiuxiwei.

(above) Traditional houses in the city show a high level of construction knowledge as evident by the presence of three and four-storey buildings.
(opposite) Homes typically have a series of courtyards. Outer courtyards are used to receive guests while inner courtyards are for family members.

土家土茯苓
茶
味纯幽香 清热解渴
减肥养颜 益寿延年

BEAUTIFUL WOOD CARVINGS OF TUJIA

COLOURFUL BATIK, BROCADE AND EMBROIDERY OF TUJIA

TUJIA PEOPLE IN WORSHIP

謝三清吉利平安

TUJIA MARRIAGE CUSTOMS

CELEBRATING WITH SONG, DANCE AND ACROBATICS

HISTORICAL BUILDINGS

(above) Memorial Hall built in honour of Marshall He Long
(opposite top) Museum built in Memory of the China Soviet Government.
(right) The route of the Long March is now a hiking trail.

中华苏维埃共
湘鄂川黔省

SUN JIANHUA

Sun Jianhua (*above*) has been a member of the Chinese Photographers Association, an esteemed national artist, a director of the Hunan Artists Association and chairman of Zhangjiajie Artists Association. Sun has pursued the Arts and photography as a professional for many years and is recognised as one of the top 10 artists within China's Hunan province. His works have been lauded in numerous national exhibitions and featured in publications such as *Collection of World Art Works*, *Contemporary Chinese Artists*, Chinese textbooks for primary and middle schools, and various compilation showcasing the works of Chinese photographers. To date, Sun has published over ten personal albums on the Arts and photography.

English text edited by Don Bosco
Project Manager (English Edition) : Melvin Neo
Designer (English Edition) : Lynn Chin Nyuk Ling
Production (English Edition) : Nor Sidah Haron

This book was first published as Miraculous Zhangjiajie by China Water Power Press in 2003.

This edition published by Times Editions – Marshall Cavendish
An imprint of Marshall Cavendish International (Asia) Private Limited
A member of the Times Publishing Limited
Times Centre, 1 New Industrial Road, Singapore 536196
Tel: (65) 6213 9300 Fax: (65) 6285 4871
E-mail: te@sg.marshallcavendish.com
Online Bookstore: www.marshallcavendish.com/genref

Malaysian Office:
Marshall Cavendish (Malaysia) Sdn Bhd (3024-D)
(General & Reference Publishing)
(Formerly known as Federal Publications Sdn Berhad)
Times Subang, Lot 46, Persiaran Teknologi Subang
Subang Hi-Tech Industrial Park
Batu Tiga, 40000 Shah Alam
Selangor Darul Ehsan, Malaysia
Tel: (603) 5635 2191, 5628 6888 Fax: (603) 5635 2706
E-mail: cchong@tpg.com.my

National Library Board Singapore Cataloguing in Publication Data
Sun, Jianhua.
Zhangjiajie: majestic mountains of Hunan, China / photography by Sun Jianhua.
— Singapore: Times Editions-Marshall Cavendish, 2004.
p. cm.
First published: China Water Power Press, 2003.
ISBN : 981-232-999-4
1. Landscape photography — China — Hunan Sheng. 2. Zhangjiajie Shi
(Hunan Sheng, China) — Pictorial works. I. Title.
TR660.5
779.3651215 — dc21 SLS2004141928

Printed in Singapore by Tien Wah Press